AFFIRMING CATHOLICISM

Michael Banner

THE PRACTICE OF ABORTION: A CRITIQUE

Series Editor: Jeffrey John

DARTON · LONGMAN + TODD

*To students past, present and future on the MA course
in Christian Ethics at King's College, London,
with gratitude for the encouragement they provide
by their enthusiasm and questions.*

First published in 1999 by
Darton, Longman and Todd Ltd
1 Spencer Court
140–142 Wandsworth High Street
London SW18 4JJ

in association with

Affirming Catholicism
St Luke's Centre
90 Central Street
London EC1V 8AQ

ISBN 0-232-52308-8

Designed and produced by Sandie Boccacci
in QuarkXPress on an Apple PowerMac
Set in 10/12$\frac{1}{2}$pt Times
Printed and bound in Great Britain by Page Brothers, Norwich

Affirming Catholicism

Affirming Catholicism is a movement (not an ecclesiastical party) which exists to do two things. We affirm our confidence in our Anglican heritage; and we seek to renew and promote the Catholic tradition within it. Our aim is to explore, explain and share with others both inside and outside the Church a lively, intelligent and inclusive Catholic faith. In the words of our Trust Deed:

> It is the conviction of many that a respect for scholarship and free enquiry has been characteristic of the Church of England and of the Churches of the wider Anglican Communion from earliest times, and is fully consistent with the status of those Churches as part of the Holy Catholic Church. It is desired to establish a charitable educational foundation which will be true both to those characteristics and to the Catholic tradition within Anglicanism ... The object of the foundation shall be the advancement of education in the doctrines and the historical development of the Church of England and the Churches of the wider Anglican Communion, as held by those standing within the Catholic tradition.

Our Publications

These are offered as one means of presenting Anglican Catholic teaching and practice in as clear and accessible a form as possible. Some cover traditional doctrinal and liturgical themes: others attempt to present a well-argued Catholic viewpoint on issues of debate currently facing the Church. There is a list of our series of booklets on page v.

The present series of books is provided, where appropriate, with summaries to sections and suggested questions which we hope will facilitate personal study or discussion in groups. Other most recent titles in the series are:

Anglican Orders and the Priesting of Women Paul Avis
Introducing Richard Hooker and The Laws of Ecclesiastical Polity
    Martyn Percy
Making a Rule of Life John Gaskell

To order these publications individually or on subscription, or for further information about the aims and activities of Affirming Catholicism, write to:

> The Secretary
> Affirming Catholicism
> St Luke's Centre
> 90 Central Street
> London EC1V 8AQ
>
> Tel: 0171 253 1138
> Fax: 0171 253 1139

Books in the Affirming
Catholicism series

About the Author

Michael Banner is F. D. Maurice Professor of Moral and Social Theology at King's College in the University of London and a priest in the Church of England. He is a member of the Royal Commission on Environmental Pollution, Chairman of the Home Office's Animal Procedures Committee, and serves on the Board for Social Responsibility and the Doctrine Commission. His most recent papers are shortly to be published under the title *Christian Ethics and Contemporary Moral Problems* (CUP).

Contents

Acknowledgements

I owe a particular debt to the Faculty of Religious Studies at McGill University in whose company I was able to spend a period of peace and quiet working on this essay during a recent sabbatical. I am most grateful for their generous hospitality, and especially that of my colleague Professor Doug Farrow. I am also grateful for the grant of study leave by the School of Humanities at King's College, London.

Germain Grisez, Colin Gunton, Paul Helm, Peter Kashouris, Oliver O'Donovan and Francis Watson read and commented on a first draft and thereby enabled me to improve it, though in some cases by trying to be more precise about certain disagreements which remain.

I. Introduction

Destruction of the embryo in the mother's womb is a violation of the right to live which God has bestowed upon this nascent life. To raise the question whether we are here concerned already with a human being or not is merely to confuse the issue. The simple fact is that God certainly intended to create a human being and that this nascent human being has been deliberately deprived of his life. And this is nothing but murder. A great many different motives may lead to an action of this kind; indeed in cases where it is an act of despair, performed in circumstances of extreme human or economic destitution and misery, the guilt may often lie rather with the community than with the individual. Precisely in this connexion money may conceal many a wanton deed, while the poor man's more reluctant lapse may far more easily be disclosed. All these considerations must no doubt have a quite decisive influence on our personal and pastoral attitude towards the person concerned, but they cannot in any way alter the fact of murder.[1]

These words of Dietrich Bonhoeffer, no matter the view we take of abortion, ought to prove somewhat shocking to contemporary Christians. The shock is not to do with his critical attitude to abortion as such, since critical attitudes, if less common than when he wrote, are still familiar enough. What will shock those familiar with the current debate amongst Christians is his view that this critical attitude is so very obviously the right and proper one as to stand in need of no extended defence. Bonhoeffer's view is straightforward and easily stated. The motives and circumstances with and in which an abortion is performed will shape our understanding of the precise quality of the action, but they cannot alter 'the simple fact' that 'this is nothing but murder'. And then, with no more than a short footnote expressing sympathy for the Roman Catholic disapproval of the killing of the foetus even in cases where the mother's life is at risk, Bonhoeffer turns to other matters.

Anyone inclined today to state as a 'simple fact' that abortion 'is nothing but murder' would very likely be dismissed out of hand, but Bonhoeffer cannot be so easily dispatched. Bonhoeffer is generally reckoned to be one of the most significant theological thinkers of his generation and even of our century. Moreover he knew well enough that there were many who did not acknowledge the 'simple fact' of the wrongness of abortion; indeed, he was writing at a time when the German State was displaying a brutal disregard for human life which the German Church had proved unable or unwilling to oppose. And yet, lacking neither skills of theological insight and argument, nor a sense of how afflicted was his own society by the moral chaos which would finally claim his own life, Bonhoeffer sees no need to develop an intricate or subtle line of argument on a matter which is in our day solemnly deemed on all sides, within and without the Church, to be difficult and perplexing – or if it is thought simple, what is thought simple is the case for rather than against abortion where the pregnancy results from rape, for example, or where the mother is herself little more than a child, or even where a baby will be 'unwanted'.

How can Bonhoeffer believe that the question of abortion is simple while knowing well enough that it is, as a matter of fact, contested? Plainly he did not subscribe to the maxim which an intellectually idle and complacent Church regularly intones where it is riven by disputes, namely that such disputes are signs of 'profound theological differences'. The existence of profound theological differences is certainly a possible explanation for disagreement, but there are plenty of others.

Disagreements in regard to almost any issue, from the most practical to the most theoretical, may have a source in such things as confusion, misinformation, inconsistency, prejudice, lack of imagination, and the like. Maybe we can, in the end, best explain a dispute within the Church by reference to 'profound theological disagreements', but we can hardly allow ourselves to presuppose the fact of such profound disagreement, when the actual character of the disagreement can only be established by attending with the utmost care and concentration to the issues before us. Disagreement there may certainly be, but its cause is a matter for discernment not presupposition.

In this essay we shall try to discern the shape and character of contemporary disagreements regarding abortion. We shall find, as a matter of fact, that the disagreement is not profound in at least two respects. In the first place, and for all its shrillness, we shall discover that the debate about abortion is marked more by certain crucial agreements than it is by radical disagreements. Furthermore and in the second place, we shall find ourselves forced to judge these agreements theologically questionable. This is to say, in other words, that the way in which the debate about abortion is framed is precisely such that its terms constrain Christian thought about abortion rather than allow its adequate expression. Insofar as it tolerates this constraint, Christian thought is captive, albeit a willing or at least unwitting captive. Thus the recovery of a Christian understanding of abortion depends on the recovery of the freedom of Christian thought from its capture by dominant modes of discussion and debate. So the merit of Bonhoeffer's simple view will emerge only as we finally see through the current debate even if we must begin our journey by entering and reviewing this debate in the terms which it allows.

II. The Current Debate

The current debate about abortion can be explored through a consideration of two related questions around which, in effect, it turns. First of all, does the status of the foetus matter and second, if it does, what is the status of the foetus?

(a) Does the Status of the Foetus Matter?

To ask the question whether the status of the foetus matters will strike many as deeply odd. Of course it must matter, it will be said, whether the foetus is, so to speak, a 'thou' or a 'that'. Isn't this why the question, for example, whether the foetus is a person is debated with such vigour?

We shall have cause to come back to that last mentioned question presently, but it is important to understand in the first place that if answers to that or similar questions do matter, they matter decisively only from certain points of view and that from other points of view, even if they do matter to some extent, they are by no means the end of debate nor even especially important to it. In particular these questions cannot be crucial for the moral theory which is known as consequentialism, and which has exerted a considerable influence in recent discussions of bioethics in particular and of public policy in general.

In popular terms consequentialism is the doctrine that the ends justify the means and is associated with the names of Bentham and Mill. (Stated more carefully it is the theory that actions are good or right, bad or wrong, in virtue, and solely in virtue, of their consequences, and further, that the morally best action in any situation is just that one which promises to maximise good consequences.) No action is as such, in and of itself, wrong. Whether or not an action is wrong is always an open or contingent question in the sense that one will in each and every case have to consider whether or not the action under consideration is likely to have, on balance, more good consequences than bad and whether it is, in particular, that one which offers the best such balance. If so, then the ends justify the means, and the consistent consequentialist will not entertain complaints which are based on the thought that there are some things which really ought not to be done no matter the good which may result – the thought which Augustine maintains when he argues that it is wrong to tell lies even for the sake of detecting heretics.[1]

Now it is easy to see that for one who approaches the issue of abortion with consequentialist assumptions, questions about the status of the foetus can have no determinative significance. Perhaps the foetus is a person and perhaps (if these are thought to be different propositions) it can be said to possess a soul. But since the killing of persons is, like any other action, always in principle on the agenda, abortion cannot just be ruled out but must always be considered amongst the repertoire of actions which may or may not contribute to the achievement of the most desirable state of affairs. Consistent exponents of such a position (and it may tell us something about the position that consistent exponents of it are sometimes hard to find) make themselves clear and understood by admitting that along with being open-minded about abortion they are necessarily and in principle open-minded about infanticide, for example.

Of course it does not follow that because consequentialists are open-minded on the subject of abortion that they will always and invariably be in favour of it. Certainly they would be suspicious of any strict prohibition of abortion, but then so ought they to be suspicious of any simply and uncritically permissive regime. There are severe problems with the sort of calculus of consequences which consequentialism presupposes. To determine that course of action, amongst all the alternatives, which offers the best balance of good and bad consequences, requires not only a remarkable ability to peer into an uncertain future, but also a not so much remarkable as questionable ability in comparing and weighing highly diverse outcomes – the problem of comparing cabbages and kings as it is sometimes characterised. But supposing for the moment and for the sake of argument that such difficulties can be surmounted – though they are considerable and arguably insurmountable – it cannot be assumed without more ado that such comparisons would favour abortion in every case in which it might be contemplated.

Certainly it seems likely that the cases which were the stuff of the campaign for law reform (the teenager who has been raped, the hard-pressed mother of an already large family expecting a handicapped child and so on) will be deemed by a consequentialist analysis to be cases where abortions are warranted – just to take the first example, the already severely traumatised young girl, probably and understandably harbouring no feelings of love for the child she never wished for, will likely be said to have but a small chance of making a good mother or of giving the child a good start in life. Whatever one makes of that claim, however – and even here one may wonder whether its truth should be taken for granted quite as readily as it seems to be – the same analysis is unlikely to seem plausible in the case of the sort of abortions which have become increasingly common and indeed routine. A couple find themselves pregnant a few years before they intended to start a family. Or alternatively, they find themselves expecting a child with a minor handicap (such as harelip). Or, to take a third case, they find the child is not of the sex they wanted (meaning, in most cases, that it is a girl and not a boy). In none of these cases does it seem likely, prima facie, that the calculation would favour abortion. Of course, the couple are in different ways disappointed. Of course, they may regard the having of a child now as something of an inconvenience. Of course, they do not presently regard the child with the tenderness and sense of expectation which they might have had for a child other than the one they find themselves with. And maybe their sense of disappointment or inconvenience may subtly (or not so subtly) affect their future relationship with the child. But to believe, even from a consequentialist viewpoint, that abortions are morally required in these cases, one would have to believe that the good which is likely to come to the child from his or her existence, however inauspicious its beginnings, and the good in addition which will come to anyone else who might care for the child in the place of the parents, is genuinely outweighed by any negative features of the case, so that on balance it would be better that the child should not be born – or at least one would have to believe, alternatively, that a greater good than would be produced by the birth of this child will come about through the birth of another that our hypothetical couple will have if they choose to have an abortion in this case but not otherwise. Now either of these beliefs seems highly dubious even if we make the handicap a good deal more severe than we have imagined it. Thus it might well be argued, though we shan't pursue the point in detail now, that even where a foetus is diagnosed as suffering from Down's Syndrome, the good of that child's existence is greater than any supposed burdens which this condition adds to the responsibilities and difficulties of parenthood. (And if this purported calculation seems to come out the other way, we would do well to pause to wonder whether the fact that the good of the child's existence is reckoned to be slight, and perhaps significantly less than that of other potential children, tells us more about the quality of care we give to the handicapped and our attitudes to them than it does about the undoubtedly objective limitations which handicap places on the possibility of human flourishing.) However that may be, in many other cases where abortions are presently sought it would seem that the good of the child's existence is greater than any disbenefits to itself or others, and thus that abortion is not warranted by consequentialist reasoning; and if that is so, it will also be that much harder to maintain as simply obvious that this good is one which is best traded for another and greater good which will result from the birth of another envisaged child. This is to overlook all such matters as the costs and traumas of abortion, the possible difficulties of conceiving, the risk that a future child might itself be severely handicapped and so on. The main point, however, is that consequentialism, often thought to provide a defence of the status quo, might well prove to be a restrictive rather than a straightforwardly permissive creed in relation to the general Western norm of abortion on demand were its recommended moral calculus attempted.

There is, of course, a respect in which the calculations we have been imagining are highly sensitive to particular elements in the situation, and this sensitivity begins to draw to our attention something of the difficulties in this whole way of thought for Christians (above and beyond the theoretical difficulties of which we must, in due course, make further mention). Suppose the various couples we have envisaged were far more deeply averse to the birth of the child they have conceived than we have imagined. Suppose, let us say, that they are so profoundly and deeply materialistic that they are utterly distraught at the possibility of their child being born before they have completed the swimming pool and games room they have always wanted to build in their garden. Or suppose that, priding themselves in particular on their looks and beauty, they find the thought of having a child with a condition as mild as harelip quite repugnant. Or suppose, in our third case, that, for whatever reason, they so value a male child over a female one, that the prospect of having a child of the 'wrong' sex causes them very significant distress. And suppose further and in each case that the consequentialist calculation is so crucially influenced or determined by these elements in the situation that they are decisive in tipping the decision against the child's life.

What this brings to our attention is that consequentialist reasoning is inclined, broadly speaking, to take our desires and wishes as fixtures and fittings, as the givens of the case which any moral calculus must take for granted. It thus invites us to stand over any situation as observers, even ones in which we are involved, making no judgement as such on the desires which are perhaps crucial in determining the character of that situation and the relative merits, in consequentialist terms, of the various possibilities for action which lie within it. But typically the stance of an uncritical observer is not one with which the conscientious thinker will feel comfortable, and Christians in particular are likely to balk at the relationship to one's desires which this stance seems to presuppose.

Two points need to be made. In the first place insofar as the consequentialist calculus seems to take our desires for granted, it overlooks the education and reordering of our desires which Christianity teaches. 'Do not be conformed to this world' says Paul, 'but be transformed by the renewal of your minds' (Romans 2:2). And this renewal of our minds, which comes about as we understand ourselves and the world in the light of the gospel of creation, reconciliation and redemption which has concerned Paul in the previous chapters of his letter, reorders our beliefs and with that reordering, reorders our attitudes, affections and desires. Thus, to go back to the cases we mentioned earlier, couples whose desire for an abortion depends on a desire for a swimming pool, for a 'perfect' child, or for a child of the 'right' sex (i.e. male), need to allow these desires to be schooled by Christian beliefs which might be expected, in different ways, to unsettle them.

But there is a second point which is important, and which comes into play even where the desires which have a part in determining the outcome of the consequentialist calculation are neither plainly, nor even arguably, disordered. Let us go back to the case of the victim of rape who finds herself pregnant. Amongst her desires variously affected by the birth of a child, might be a desire to go to university, or to take up a new and demanding job abroad, or to give more time to her writing, music or art. None of these desires is, on the face of it, improper. Even in a life which is in a very high degree morally conscientious, we might expect that such desires could and would and even should be satisfied in some way. But there is still something wrong, Christians might feel, with the invitation which consequentialism makes to us, even when our desires are the vital factors in the situation, to adopt the stance of observers and discern the best outcome by weighing in the balance the satisfaction of our desires alongside the satisfaction of any others. Bentham's famous slogan 'each to count for one and no more than one' is a proper plea against the temptation to which all moral agents are prone of thinking that their happiness should count for more simply on account of its being theirs! But the neutrality about my own happiness which prevents me counting it twice, becomes questionable when it seems to prevent me from wondering whether in some circumstances I should consider counting it less than once. Of course when I am told that a decision favouring the claims of **a** over **b** will produce the best balance of consequences, I shall, if I think in consequentialist terms, favour this decision over any others. Even when I discover that I am **b**, I shall if I am properly disinterested, continue to hold that this is the best outcome. But the minute that I discover that I am **a**, I immediately find myself invited, though not by consequentialism, to occupy another and different position and perspective, in which the fact of my being an agent possessed of moral responsibility asks me to consider whether my desires should count for less than one. (And this is why what are often called 'pastoral approaches' to moral problems are so insufferably patronising, bidding me abandon the perspective of a moral agent for whom sacrifice is a genuine moral option and for whom the distinction between what is forgivable or understandable on the one hand, and what is right on the other, remains important.) None of this, of course, settles the question of what course of action the victim of rape should follow; it is to say, however, that there are certain further questions she may well wish to pose in spite of consequentialism, which simply refuses them.

We have been giving the consequentialist approach a run for its money, granting for the sake of argument its highly controversial assumption that, broadly speaking, ends may justify means and also its equally controversial assumptions concerning the possibility of a moral calculus. We have seen how this approach will tend to shape our thinking about the problem of abortion, though we have also seen that a consistent consequentialism can by no means be assumed to be conservative in relation to the present permissive regime. But we have further seen that, even prior to examining its basic assumptions directly, we discover problems with consequentialism as we consider its failure properly to account for two aspects of moral thought in relation to our desires which Christians, but not only Christians, will wish to highlight: in the first place that these desires may need 'schooling', and in the second place, even where they do not, that the responsibilities of moral agency seem to invite us to adopt a relationship towards them more subtle than unthinking neutrality. In both cases what seems wrong is the tendency to stand outside the situation as mere observers, on the one hand treating desires as givens beyond reform, and on the other forgetting that some of the desires which constrain the situation are ours.

It is high time, however, to ask some questions about the key assumption from which consequentialism begins. We have already mentioned Augustine's insistence that it is wrong to tell lies even for the sake of detecting heretics. In making this claim Augustine appeals in the first instance to the authority of

Paul ('You should not do evil that good may come', Romans 3:8), but this appeal to authority does not prevent him developing a case which anticipates many of the arguments which have featured in modern-day disputes regarding the validity of consequentialism. In the end, however, Augustine's case against those who would tell lies for a good purpose comes down to this: to hold that it is sometimes right to lie is to hold that one may do evil that good may come; but this is to hold that if of the 'number of lewd Priscillianists [the heretics in question], some woman should cast her eye upon a catholic Joseph, and promise him she will betray their hidden retreats if she obtain from him that he lie with her, and it be certain that if he consent unto her she will make good her promise', we would be obliged to conclude that he should 'lie with her', so that there would be 'chaste adulteries', or thefts, or blasphemies, or whatever may be necessary to achieve the good end. But this, thinks Augustine, is absurd. Though 'It does indeed make very much difference, for what cause, with what end, with what intention a thing be done ... those things which are clearly sins, are upon no plea of a good cause, with no seeming good end, no alleged good intention, to be done.'[2]

What is the force of this argument? Isn't it simply, someone might say, an insistence that 'one should not do evil that good may come?' when this is exactly what is in dispute between consequentialism and its critics? The form of Augustine's argument here is that of a *reductio ad absurdum*, whereby the implications of a belief (in this case the belief that one may do evil that good may come and the implication that there might be good thefts, fornications and blasphemies) are held up as absurd. Now those thus challenged can, in principle, make a number of replies. They might maintain that the alleged implications of the fundamental principle, whether or not they are absurd, are not in fact implications of it. This, however, does not seem to be a promising strategy in this particular case. Alternatively, if it is conceded that the implications really are implications, it will have to be contended that they are by no means absurd. Sure enough, it may be admitted, it seems surprising that there can be good thefts, fornications and blasphemies, but surprising conclusions are not the same as absurd ones.

The shift in moral opinion since Augustine's time, however motivated, does not help him here and in presenting his argument to an audience of modern-day undergraduates (even perhaps to an audience of ordinands) one would probably be well advised to change his examples, since perceptions of various elements of the real and imagined cases have changed. Thus catching heretics is perhaps not thought to be a very pressing good end, and more to the point, the existence of good thefts, and possibly even of good fornications and blasphemy, may be thought obvious rather than absurd. But the particular examples don't matter of course, for the principle that one may do evil that good may come will also yield the conclusion that, say, one may, for the sake of a greater good, discriminate against someone on ground of race or sex, that one might torture children, or that one might commit rape. And those conclusions are perhaps as likely to seem absurd to many moderns, as Augustine's examples seemed to many of his contemporaries.

Still, however, the determined defender of consequentialism may refuse to concede. Consequentialism is a moral theory which understands very well that its conclusions will seem absurd, and thus that its acceptance will lead to a reform of moral practice. It is hardly surprising that its conclusions will be opposed and resisted, its advocates will insist, but they are by no means shown to be wrong by such opposition.

The nature of this opposition must, however, be understood, since it can give an account of itself as something other than mere resistance to new ideas. Augustine's argument is, in essence and to translate it into our terms, that if consequentialism maintains that actions are good or bad solely in virtue of their consequences, then no action is, in principle, illicit. But, contrary to such an assumption, so Augustine and his modern allies claim, the belief that rape, racial discrimination and torturing children are always and ever wrong, is more certain than any claim about actions being justified by their consequences. That claim is, after all, a theoretical judgement which is itself neither self-evident nor supported by manifestly compelling argument. And even if the theoretical claim were better supported, so they might continue, at the least it has to be admitted that the relationship between moral theory and moral practice is more complex than any automatic favouring of the theoretical predilections of consequentialism seems to allow.

Take an analogy. Someone proposes a theory of what makes for good drama. On paper it looks a simple and persuasive account. But when we start to apply this dramatic theory to plays we know, we find that it does not so much modify, deepen or nuance our critical judgements (which any good theory surely will) but radically overthrows them. Thus we find that according to this theory, *Henry V*, *Romeo and Juliet* and *Hamlet* are all to be reckoned bad plays; so too, let us suppose, the entire works of Racine, Chekov and Molière. Now there is nothing here to compel the advocate of the theory to withdraw; like a government minister whose position has become 'unsustainable' as the press has it, the theorist may just 'tough it out'. It will, however, take a very strong preference for theory over practice for the theorist to stick to his or her guns and insist that these really are bad plays when the application of the theory is more likely to encourage us to wonder about its adequacy. For surely we properly trust our first order judgements about what counts as a good play (even if we don't think these judgements are infallible), more than we trust any second order theories about drama – which is just to say that our sense that *Hamlet* is a great play is considerably more secure than any theory about the nature of drama which we might spin.

Now the point of this analogy is to suggest the following. The claim that we may do evil that good may come is itself a second order, theoretical judgement. But this claim comes into conflict with all sorts of first order moral judgements: such as that one should not torture children, discriminate on grounds of race or sex, or whatever. There is, however, no reason to be forced into an abandonment of these first order judgements by a second order theory, which is itself less secure than those judgements. Indeed there is every reason to refuse to be bullied by this unwarranted preference for theory over practice, albeit that one must rightly allow that the relationship between theory and practice in this area is a matter of some subtlety and needs careful handling. The problem with consequentialism, however, is just that it seems unaware of any such subtleties.

Although we haven't mentioned abortion for a while, the discussion has been far from irrelevant to our subject. We began by asking the perhaps surprising question whether, in thinking about abortion, the status of the foetus matters. We pointed out that for the moral theory which holds that the ends justify the means, the status of the foetus could never be of decisive significance. It must always be an open question whether an abortion is justified in the circumstances, whether or not the foetus is a person, just because the killing of persons is itself always a possible course of action according to this point of view. We have sought to show, however, that there are certain good reasons for not accepting consequentialism, or at the least that its claims to our allegiance are far from obvious; hence the question of the status of the foetus becomes important, for the very reason that the taking of the life of a foetus might just be one of those means which no ends would justify. So the question of the status of the foetus cannot, it seems, be avoided.

Someone might still be forgiven for supposing that although not irrelevant in principle, the discussion has been something of a diversion in fact, just because apart from in departments of philosophy (or more commonly in departments of economics) consequentialists are rarely to be met with. Such a degree of intellectual quarantine would doubtless have been desirable, but the fact is that consequentialism has played a considerable role in shaping discussion about a host of moral questions even where those who seem to rely upon its pre-suppositions would be incapable of identifying or naming it. Thus one may discern the influence of consequentialism in the debate about abortion, as elsewhere, even when its assumptions are neither explicitly acknowledged nor adequately defended. Two examples will illustrate why the preceding discussion has been vital.

The first example will be recognised by anyone who has ever discussed the subject of abortion and has indicated even a passing willingness to entertain the thought that abortion is morally wrong as such and therefore should not enter into our thinking as an acceptable means to certain ends, no matter how good those ends may be. The defender of the status quo who refuses to give this thought a moment's reflection will certainly gain rhetorical advantage by decrying the 'ex-tremism' of his or her opponents, and may even press the advantage by labelling their attitude 'absolutist'. And if this is not enough to win the day, one can develop the argument (one uses the noun loosely) by contrasting a 'negative absolutism' with an 'affirming pragmatism'; in some circles one can suc-cessfully round the whole thing off by further characterising the 'negative absolutism' as 'papist', though it is always as well to deploy this further refinement with a little caution for fear of sacrificing the advantage thus far gained with any who might harbour Roman Catholic prejudices.[3]

Of course this will not do. The labels 'extremist' and 'absolutist' are certainly ones which no one will pick to describe their own position, but it is by no means clear that the rhetorical advantage which is gained by pressing these labels on those who think that abortion may be wrong in principle is anything other than rhetorical. After all, to revert to the earlier discussion, the committed consequentialist who thinks that non-therapeutic and harmful experimentation on unwilling human subjects may be justified can equally accuse all those who support the Nuremberg Code of being 'absolutists' and 'extremists', though it may be more difficult to make the label 'papist' stick in this case. Anyone *but* a consequentialist will be an absolutist in relation to certain moral principles, even if they disagree with some others about the scope of those principles – thus to change the example, it is hardly helpful, intellectually speaking, to accuse the out and out pacifist of being an 'absolutist' if one wishes to maintain oneself that, let us say, the killing of prisoners of war is wrong. One might conclude, then, that the abolition of the label 'absolutist', while it would deprive some of a crutch, would serve the purposes of all those who are concerned that these matters should be subject to rational argument rather than to the crudest of rhetorical tricks.

If the use of the charge of 'absolutism' is typically an evasion which could only become something other than that by an acknowledged reliance on consequentialism and a willingness to defend its presuppositions, so too is the use of the slogan which asserts 'a woman's right to choose' if it is deployed as a bar to debate and not, as it might be, as a statement of a conclusion arrived at by means of an argument which can be brought out into the open, explicated and defended. On the face of it the slogan is no more than an assertion by members of a particular group of a claim to be entitled to act in this matter as they alone determine; it is as if, that is to say, a case against slavery were met with the assertion of 'a slave-owner's right to choose'. But in either case, a discussion of the rights and wrongs of who should take decisions in these matters presupposes that whatever is being chosen is the sort of thing which can properly be chosen, when that is just what is in question where the status of the slave or the foetus is a matter for dispute. And if consequentialism is unacceptable, the rightness or wrongness of choosing an abortion will crucially depend on the answer to the question which we must now address: what is the status of the foetus?

(b) What Is the Status of the Foetus?

For many the question of the status of the foetus is where the debate about abortion really begins. Not only have they never heard of consequentialism, but they are not attracted by its doctrines. They will presuppose – and, so we have claimed, may presuppose with a certain propriety – that there are certain sorts of actions which ought not to be done no matter the intentions and ends one might have in view in doing them. Now we have already noted in mentioning Augustine, that different individuals and societies may give different lists of such actions, but one likely candidate for inclusion in any list of 'thou shalt nots' is a 'thou shalt not kill'. Stated positively, many people would say that human life is sacred, and that its sacredness requires that it be accorded absolute respect. It is certainly right in general to consider the consequences of our actions, they might say, but never right to take human life even for the sake of very good consequences.

We can hardly fail to notice, however, that the 'thou shalt not kill' with which our society is most familiar occurs in the law code of a nation which eschewed neither war nor capital punishment. It would be a mistake to conclude too quickly that this is a blatant inconsistency; the very fact of its blatancy renders such an explanation somewhat unlikely. Indeed it is better to suppose quite simply that 'thou shalt not kill' was understood rather more specifically than it is by those who take the view that the prohibition precludes both war and capital punishment. Maybe it was understood, that is to say, as prohibiting the killing of the innocent, for example, and thus as perfectly consistent with the practices mentioned.

It is not to the point to pursue the question as to which of these or other construals of the commandment is to be preferred. That there is a question to be pursued, however, points to the fact that a dispute about the rights and wrongs of abortion should not immediately be characterised as a dispute between those who accept and those who deny a doctrine of the sanctity of human life. Certainly we have seen that this way of characterising the situation will sometimes be appropriate: the consistent and hard-nosed consequentialist is, of course, obliged to deny any doctrine of the sanctity of human life just because such a doctrine would hold that human life (or innocent human life) is to be accorded an absolute respect. But the example of the previous paragraph suggests that there can be a dispute about the principle of the sanctity of human life even between those who accept it, a dispute not about its validity, that is to say, but about its scope. Thus those who argue that the foetus (or the foetus up to twenty-four weeks, prior to viability, or at whatever other point) falls outside the scope of the principle, like those who argue that convicted murderers fall outside its scope, are not to be accused immediately of doubting the validity of the principle as such. Indeed, one way of making sense of the law in relation to abortion in most Western jurisdictions is just to see it as ruling on the scope whilst not questioning the validity of the principle of the sanctity of human life, since these jurisdictions typically signal a continuing commitment to that principle by leaving in place the crime of infanticide, for example.

The current and predominant legal position and its advocates and defenders cannot, then, be accused of simply denying the doctrine of the sanctity of human life; their position may make moral sense precisely in terms of the distinction between validity and scope to which we have alluded. Of course, it may not make moral sense. It may emerge that as a matter of fact there is a hidden inconsistency in the proposal to exclude foetuses, so that what should be treated in the first instance as a claim about the scope of the principle can, on second sight and after closer examination, be held to be a surreptitious rejection of it. That is to say that there are some attempts to establish the scope or bounds of a principle which have finally to be considered repudiations of it, since the case for the limitation is not morally comprehensible.

We could mark and illustrate the difference by contrasting the explication of a rule with the mere making of exceptions to it. Thus the rule that 'no pets are permitted within the college grounds' is explicated when we learn that guide dogs are permitted within the college, since we discover that the word 'pets' is construed, perfectly reasonably, as not covering certain working animals. But if we learn that the bursar's dog is permitted in the college we have not so much better understood the principle as simply learnt of an exception which, for whatever reason, is made to it. The exception is not completely mysterious, since the role and influence of bursars is generally such that we are not exactly surprised that it is made; but its existence is not explicable by reference to the rule's underlying rationale and is thus not, so to speak, morally comprehensible, and hence amounts to a repudiation of the rule, albeit one which may not threaten its general effectiveness.

Returning to the dispute about the scope of the principle of the sanctity of human life, we must give notice, then, that whilst we shall endeavour to treat the dispute as just that (that is, as a dispute about the proper explication of the rule between those who accept its validity), a failure to make moral sense of any proffered 'explications' will drive us to consider whether limitations of the rule's scope in relation to the foetus must, in fact, be deemed mere exceptions. To be specific, we may find ourselves forced to conclude that the limitations which are placed on the scope of the principle of the sanctity of life by the exclusion of foetuses from the protection it is usually reckoned to afford, are not morally compelling, however else they may be motivated.

One way in which the limitation is held to be justified is, of course, by maintaining that the protection which the principle requires is owed to persons, but that foetuses (or at least foetuses prior to viability, or whatever) are not persons and therefore are not within the principle's scope. Thus the question as to whether or not the limitation on the scope of the principle is acceptable is converted into the question 'is the foetus a person?'

It is, however, by no means obvious that the conversion of the question into this form actually constitutes a step towards its resolution. It could only constitute such a step if there were agreement not only on the principle that absolute respect is owed only to persons (which we may assume for the sake of argument), but also on the further and rather crucial matter of what it is to be a person, or at least on how this further question could be settled. And yet on both these points – on what it is to be a person, and on how the question of what it is to be a person could be settled – unanimity is not to be found.

On the question of what it is to be a person we find on one side the view that from the moment of conception we have to do with a living and independent being (independent in the sense that it cannot be regarded as a part of the mother's body), the life of which can only be human; now since all humans are persons, the newly fertilised egg or embryo is a person. On the other side we find the view that whilst the foetus is certainly alive and its life is human life, not all humans are persons. Typically it will be said that to be a person is to exercise certain functions and capacities characteristic of human life: it might be, for example, that the exercise of rational choice (which is what is usually meant by possession of autonomy) is picked out as the defining characteristic. Now a foetus is not capable of rational choice and is, therefore, not a person. (Obviously there are numerous variations on these two positions.)

Though both sides claim to agree that protection and respect is owed to persons, since they differ over what it is to be a person, this posing of the problem of abortion in these terms will only represent an advance if we have some means of agreeing on which of these accounts of what it is to be a person is to be preferred. No advance will be achieved whilst one side deduces from one set of premises (including the premise that all human beings are persons) that foetuses fall under the scope of the protection which the principle of the sanctity of life extends to persons, whilst the other side deduces from another set of premises (including the premise that only those presently capable of rational choice are persons) that they do not. But it is by no means obvious what these means would be; plainly it would be ridiculous to suppose that resort to a dictionary will allow us to choose between the two key premises (even if it provides evidence of what people have traditionally thought about the denotation of the word 'person'), since those who say that the foetus is or is not a person are not making a claim about how words are used, but rather about how they should be used. They are saying, in other words, that the word 'person', which is typically employed to mark out a subject of legal and moral standing, should or should not apply to the foetus. But the force of the 'should' in either case depends not on facts about language, but on facts concerning the foetus. Thus the debate is more helpfully posed not by asking ourselves whether the foetus is or is not a person, but by asking whether there is any difference or differences between the foetus and those human beings held uncontroversially worthy of protection by the principle of the sanctity of life which would render the denial of that same protection to the foetus morally explicable.

Of course, as has been said, there are any number of different candidates as answers to this question, some of which we have already encountered. We might think of these answers as on a continuum with the most exclusive answers at one end, and with the more inclusive at the other. Arranging them in these terms, some popular attempts to identify a difference which makes a difference, so to speak, might be rationality, twenty-four weeks or viability, sentience or the capacity to feel pain, or fourteen days. We should look at each of these, albeit briefly, in turn.

The notion that because it lacks rationality the foetus is properly denied the protection which the principle of the sanctity of life demands in other cases has a certain simplicity to it, and also latches on to one aspect of certain common ways of thinking about the respect due to life in its different forms. Thus whatever view we may take about experimentation on animals, for example, most people would, at the very least, prefer that animals other than higher primates should be used where this is possible. This preference may have a number of roots, but one might lie in the sense that the relatively rich mental life of which chimpanzees, for example, are thought capable, renders their use objectionable where other animals would serve the purpose.

What this may suggest to us (though it would require a good deal more analysis and discussion if it were to do more than suggest it) is that the wrongness of taking a life may increase in proportion to the mental richness of that life. But even if it does suggest this, it is one thing to suggest that the possession of rationality may increase the wrongness of killing, and quite another to show that its absence could serve to excuse it in some cases or more generally to render it innocent. On the last point, not everything which seems to be deserving of respect and protection is rational, or even alive, or even for that matter presently in existence. Animals, plants, landscapes, eco-systems, works of art, historic buildings, corpses and future generations are just some of the items which it can be argued make claims, in different ways, for respect and protection;[4] and if this is so, it is by no means obvious that foetuses (not to mention newborn infants, the severely mentally handicapped and the senile, since these too may be held to lack rationality) can properly be treated as disqualified from moral regard simply because they lack rationality.

Lack of rationality may, however, be thought to warrant not

complete disqualification from moral consideration, but simply disqualification from the absolute protection which is accorded by the principle of the sanctity of life. After all it might be said, the fact that lots of things lacking rationality have a certain moral standing does not show that they should be accorded the moral standing normally attributed to human life. Rationality, it might be admitted, is not the foundation for all moral standing, but is precisely the foundation for the specific form of moral standing which is expressed by the principle that one should not intend the death of a human being, whereas one might, in certain circumstances and without denying their moral standing completely, intend the death or destruction of an animal, plant, building, and so on.

This claim – that rationality is a necessary condition for possessing the moral standing recognised by the principle of the sanctity of life – plainly has more to be said for it than the wider claim that rationality is a necessary condition for moral standing as such. It is not clear, however, that this more is enough to compel its acceptance. In the first place, it seems to overlook a fact of arguably some importance, namely that the foetus will, unlike animals, plants and buildings, come to possess the rationality typically associated with human life. In the second place, however, this stipulation of a condition necessary to gain the absolute protection normally accorded to human life (i.e. present possession of certain rational faculties) deprives, as we have said, the senile, the severely mentally handicapped and the newborn of such protection. But it suffers from a further difficulty just in the fact of its being a stipulation; for whilst it may be that one cannot oblige someone, by appeal to universally accepted reasons, not to make this stipulation supposing they are willing to accept its implications, the fact is, however, that alongside it stand countless other possible stipulations, perhaps more exclusive (an IQ in excess of 100, for example) which seem to share with it its seemingly morally arbitrary character.

The drawing of the line at viability – commonly said to be attained presently at twenty-four weeks, though arguably attained earlier than this already, and certainly to be expected to be attained ever earlier as medicine develops – has a strong claim from the medical or legal point of view at least in the sense that if a line is to be drawn, it should certainly be drawn no later than this. If it were to be drawn later, then depending on the method of abortion, highly anomalous situations would arise, whereby a foetus could be delivered alive in one part of a hospital and left to die, where in another part of the hospital the same conduct might not only be considered as constituting bad medical practice but might also give rise to a charge of murder or manslaughter. The key difference between these cases would lie, presumably, in the wishes of the mother, but reference to parental wishes is hardly a secure or principled reference point for good medical practice or for the law of murder; thus viability commends itself as a place at or before which a line should be drawn.

The reasons for saying that if a line is to be drawn anywhere it should not be drawn any later than at this point in the foetus's development are not however, in themselves, reasons for saying that it should not be drawn earlier (or not at all). And whilst the moment of viability has, as we have noted, a certain legal and medical utility, it is far from clear that viability has any moral relevance, let alone decisive moral significance. As regards its significance, all sorts of people are 'viable' only through their reliance on others, even if this reliance is not as intimate or extensive as the reliance of a foetus on its mother. It is hard to see how a failure to have reached the moment of viability should exclude foetuses from the protection of the principle of the sanctity of life, without also excluding these others, but more to the point it is even harder to see why viability should count at all. Again it is open to someone to stipulate that life can be taken with impunity where it cannot be sustained without assistance, or, more modestly, that such life does not deserve absolute protection even if it deserves some moral consideration; but though these creeds have certainly had an appeal for some of our century's more notorious regimes, it is far from obvious that weakness is to be regarded as disqualifying human life from protection.

The acquisition of a capacity for pain is sometimes held to be the point at which to draw a line. (The dating of this point is a matter of uncertainty and controversy which need not concern us; many would argue that twenty-three weeks is the likely stage at which the foetus develops the capacity for pain without thereby ruling out entirely the possibility that it may be gained much earlier indeed.[5]) But again, as with rationality, the identification of a capacity for pain as *the* morally significant moment seems to confuse what may increase culpability with what is necessary to it. Certainly the fact that a being suffers in its death is a factor in our assessment of the exact moral character of the killing, just as is its capacity for various forms of intellectual and social life. But a killing can plainly be wrongful even where no pain is suffered. Thus the fact that the foetus does not feel pain cannot thereby be sufficient to show that its death is not a subject for moral criticism, nor even that while the foetus has some moral standing it does not deserve the protection accorded by the principle of the sanctity of human life.

Perhaps it makes a difference, however, that the early foetus rather than simply not feeling pain, is in fact incapable of feeling pain. The point would be that the foetus's incapacity in this respect serves to indicate that it is not a sentient being; thus, while it may be true that a killing can be wrongful even where no pain is suffered, it might be argued that it is wrongful, even though painless, just because the killing ends a sentient life. Where there is no pain because there is no sentience, so it might be said, the killing is not wrongful.

The problems with this argument seem to be twofold. In the first place, we can repeat in part the point we made in relation to the claim that rationality should function as a criterion of moral significance. Although sentience is, so to speak, a lower hurdle than rationality, it is still the case that as we review the list we gave then of things which might be held to make moral claims upon us without being rational we find some which are not sentient: plants, works of art and corpses, for example. Thus it is far from obvious that the foetus does not deserve protection just because it lacks sentience. In any case, and in the second place, the foetus will possess sentience supposing it develops. Of course, if I were to kill it in the meantime I would have deprived the foetus only of a potential for sentience, but that defence of my actions seems weak, since we usually reckon it wrong to deprive people of capacities they will possess in the future, even if they do not possess them now. (It would be no defence to the charge that one had removed an eight-year-old girl's ovaries to insist that one had done her no harm since one had merely deprived her of her potential fertility.) But a deeper problem with sentience as a criterion for moral regard can be brought out by noticing another item on our earlier list: future generations. The nature of any obligation we may owe to future generations is a matter of some debate, but without going into that question we can at least remark that if we do owe an obligation to future generations (as current commitments to sustainable development, for example, suppose), it cannot be their present capacities which ground this obligation, since they have no present capacities. But then if we do have an obligation to future generations in spite of their lacking present capacities including sentience, it is difficult to understand how the early foetus's lack of sentience should disqualify it from moral regard. It has a potential for sentience and for rationality in a much more straightforward sense than do non-existent future generations: if allowed to go to term a viable foetus will possess all those capacities we associate with fully developed human beings. Of course if we kill the foetus now it will be none the wiser and will never come to regret our actions. But if we could not defend ourselves against the charge that our present lifestyle threatens future generations by pointing out that we intend to live in such a manner that there will be no future generations, it is unclear why the same defence should be contemplated in the case of the foetus.

The difficulties even with as relatively inclusive a criterion as sentience must drive us to consider the claims made for fourteen days as the point at which what would now generally be referred to as an embryo rather than a foetus, should be afforded the protection of the principle of the sanctity of life. Such claims deserve our attention for two reasons. In the first place, although abortions typically occur much later than this, the question of the moral acceptability of abortions prior to fourteen days is a pertinent issue since its determination will be relevant to the acceptability of what are often thought of as forms of contraception but which either plainly ('morning-after' pills and chemical 'contraceptives', such as RU486) or generally (the IUD, or 'coil' as it is sometimes known) function as abortifacients. In the second place, the fourteen-day divide has assumed a certain significance as the point at which UK and other law prohibits experimentation on embryos, and if we are to make moral sense of the present legal settlement we shall need to reckon with this feature of the law as well as with the law relating to abortion as such.

Those who take the view that prior to fourteen days the embryo is not deserving of the protection demanded by the principle of the sanctity of human life tend to be impressed by a number of features of early embryonic development.

(a) Until about fourteen days it remains unclear whether early embryos will actually go on to become individual human beings – a particular embryo may become two (as in the case of monozygotic twins) or none (if it develops as a hydatidiform mole).

(b) Whilst the embryo is genetically unique from conception, and may be developmentally unique, so to speak, from around fourteen days, it is still a relatively undifferentiated organism, and certainly lacks many of the capacities we associate with fully developed human life, such as sentience.

(c) It seems that as few as one in five fertilised eggs actually develops to term. Furthermore many of those which are unsuccessful are genetically abnormal.

The significance of these considerations is by no means uncontroversial, however, and replies could be made as follows.

(a) The uncertainty about whether an early embryo will go on to become an individual human being or will become two or none, is just that: an uncertainty. In the present state of scientific knowledge we do not know what the outcome of the development of a particular embryo will be. It is, however, odd to argue from our uncertainty about whether something is true (i.e. whether the early embryo will finally become an individual human being) to its being false (i.e. that the early embryo is not an individual human being) or to its being permissible for us to act as if it were false.

(b) The fact that the early embryo is relatively undifferentiated and does not yet possess the capacities which we typically associate with fully developed human beings is not obviously significant for reasons we have previously explored.

(c) It is difficult to see what, if any, significance should be attached to the natural wastage of early embryos or to the fact that many so lost are genetically impaired. The fact that infant mortality has often stood at very high levels, especially so in the case of the handicapped, does not cause us to doubt our duty to respect the sanctity of infant life in general, nor the sanctity of the life of the handi-capped in particular.

Now those who are utterly convinced of the case for the moral significance of the fourteen-day divide could claim to behave conscientiously in supporting the practice of abortion and the use of abortifacients up to this point and no further. But it is extremely difficult to see what basis such utter conviction could have, since the replies to points (a), (b) and (c) are, at the least, grounds for thinking that the matter is unproven. Thus a proper moral caution would seem to require that we make use of neither, for if the killing of a foetus is possibly wrong that possibility argues against killing, rather than providing a justification for it.

Am I claiming then, someone might ask, that abortion is always morally wrong and furthermore that it can be shown to be such by argument? The first half of the question had better be left until we have examined what the tradition has considered hard cases, but the second half of the question can be answered here and now. Looking back over the discussion, it will be seen that what has been maintained is that there are no differences between the foetus and those human beings typically held worthy of protection by the principle of the sanctity of life which are both morally relevant and plainly morally sufficient to justify making an exception of the foetus; that is to say, no differences which would render the denial of that same protection to the foetus fully morally explicable. This denial seems to be an arbitrary repudiation of the principle, then, rather than a morally comprehensible ex-plication of its scope. So much argument can show. But were we to confront someone who denies the principle altogether it is clear that the appeal to consistency on which the argument thus far has depended can do no further work for us. When, for example, a modern philosopher (echoing Nietzsche) describes 'the idea of human dignity' as the 'moral effluvium of a discredited metaphysics',[6] the error, if there is one, is not one of logic alone. There is no inconsistency here, but rather the consistent application of a metaphysics and anthropology (i.e. a view of the world and humankind) which repudiates the valuation of human life, and individual human life, which belongs within, for example, the Christian tradition.

Karl Barth wrote:

> The last war, with all that led up to it and all its possible consequences, has posed afresh the problem of humanity from the particular angle of the question of the rights, dignity and sanctity of the fellow-man. Humanity stands at the crossroads. In its future development as humanity, will it be for man or against him? Behind the political, social and economic possibilities there stands always with the same urgency, if in different forms, the necessity of this decision.[7]

What Barth and Nietzsche both believed, for all their differences, is that that decision will only be made for the 'rights, dignity and sanctity of the fellow-man' if it takes its stand on a 'discredited metaphysics'.

We wondered to begin with whether we might make sense of the law in relation to abortion as it stands in most Western jurisdictions by seeing it as ruling on the scope whilst not questioning the validity of a principle of respect for human life, since these jurisdictions typically signal a commitment to that principle by continuing to criminalise infanticide, for example. But recall that in pursuing answers to the question 'what is the status of the foetus?', we have failed to make moral sense of the various grounds which might be offered as justifying exclusion of the foetus from the protection typically accorded to human life. Some of these grounds seemed morally irrelevant. Thus, although the foetus is not viable, this fact about it seems beside the point – one might as well say that it is small. Other grounds seem morally relevant, but not decisive; certainly the early foetus is not sentient, but sentience is arguably necessary neither for moral consideration in general nor for the particular moral consideration enshrined in the principle of the sanctity of life. When we add in the prohibition of experimentation on embryos after fourteen days the scene becomes more complicated, since if it is wrong to experiment on embryos after fourteen days it is far from plain how it can be right to abort them up to twenty-four weeks, unless we can make ourselves believe that the status of a foetus and its claim to protection are crucially determined by whether it is in a glass dish or in the womb. The law, and the medical practice it permits, presents a morally confused picture, which could, as we have acknowledged, be rendered consistent by a move in either direction, either for or against the foetus. Sometimes then, as Barth also observed, we may find ourselves giving thanks to God for the inconsequence of humankind.

III. Beyond the Current Debate

So far we have reviewed the debate about abortion in the terms in which it is commonly conducted. But we have already indicated that in these terms the argument is wrongly posed; thus the simple view taken by Bonhoeffer will commend itself to us not as a conclusion to that argument, but only as we come to understand why this way of framing the questions is, from a Christian viewpoint, highly problematic. The Church has no business simply entering this debate on the terms which the debate itself allows, just because, as we shall see, those terms do not facilitate the statement of the Church's distinctive point of view.

Though the debate about abortion can sometimes seem quite varied and complex, the sense of diversity is diminished when we take note of the fact that it is commonly characterised and thought about, and with some legitimacy, as a debate between essentially two positions which are identified by means of labels which serve as shorthand indications for the sets of assumptions, arguments and counter-arguments which we have outlined: 'pro-choice' and 'pro-life'. As we have seen, the pro-choice position, if it is to understand itself as rational and defensible rather than as a mere assertion of an unargued preference, is likely to depend on one or other of two leading assumptions (and, in addition, of course, on a number of sub-ordinate arguments or claims). Either it must assume, with consequentialism, that the question of the status of the foetus is not decisive, since the best action is simply that which maximises good consequences, or, declining that route, it must assume that the foetus is not in fact deserving of moral consideration, or, if deserving of moral consideration, is not deserving of the absolute respect which would make it wrong to intend its death, but only of a moral consideration which seems to give way before any contrary claims. Thus the mother has a right to choose. The pro-life position, on the other hand, will contest these claims and argue that the mother's rights, whatever they may be, cannot include a right to deprive another of his or her most basic right, namely the right to life.

From the point of view of the Church, however, there is a danger that these two positions could come to represent false options, even though the second is often advocated by those with sincere and strong Christian convictions. The danger is just that the affirmations of the pro-life case come to be determined to a certain extent by the denials of the pro-choice party, or at the least that the pro-life case will be interpreted in the terms of the pro-choice case to which it is dialectically related. In either case what is distinctive and important in a Christian understanding of human life may be lost in this particular exchange (and especially so when the advocates of the pro-life position may think it prudent to present their case as being independent of any particular or acknowledged Christian convictions). To be more specific, since the pro-choice position regards the child as needing (but failing) to establish certain claims against the mother, the pro-life position may seem to take its stand on the existence of just such a legitimate claim, characterised as a right to life. But in seeming to concede the requirement laid down in the pro-life argument, and in meeting it with an assertion of the right to life, important Christian convictions are at risk of being lost.

The pro-choice conviction that a particular human life must, so to say, justify itself, calls into question the fundamental conviction that human life is a good and a gift of God. To take a critical attitude towards the foetus and to ask that it prove itself, and in general to regard humanity as an achievement or qualification and not as a simple and natural endowment, is to dispute this conviction, and to doubt the justification which human life has in its creation and redemption by God. (And although the doubt is directed at another, and not at me, it is hard to see how the doubt, once active, can be contained; thus, to take the most immediate case, for a mother to adopt such a critical stance towards her own child seems to take a despising of the created order as close to a despising of the self as one can come without falling into the utter despair of self-hatred. For in this case it becomes clear that the alienation of self from other against which the command to love our enemies is directed, takes on a new and particularly stark form when even one's own child is found in the place of the stranger and enemy needing to rely on this command for its protection, a form in which the alienation of the self from other is on the verge of converting into a simple alienation from the self.)

Since, however, the assumption that the child needs to establish some particular claim is problematic, the assertion of the existence of a valid claim on the other side will be problematic in itself, regardless of the nature of the claim which is made. In addition, however, the particular claim which is in fact made on behalf of the child is, from a Christian point of view, dubious even though it aims at the child's protection. For the appeal to a 'right to life' not only seems to concede the need for justification, but does so by appealing to a certain regard for life which can have no basis in Christian thought. According to Barth, 'Everywhere life itself and as such is regarded as the actual ethical lord, teacher and master of man. ... In theological ethics the concept of life cannot be given this tyrannical and totalitarian function.'[1] For theological ethics, that is to say, life is not itself the ethical lord, but the gift of the Lord in whose service life is properly spent, and spent in two senses. Suicide is wrong just because it refuses to spend life in the service of God. Martyrdom is right just because it is willing to spend life, in a different sense, in the service of God. The rightness of spending life in the service of God, in the double sense, means, plainly enough, that what is crucial to a Christian understanding of life is not that life must always and ever be protected and served, but rather that life must always and ever be regarded not as our own, but as belonging to God. Against this understanding of human existence, insistence on a 'right to life' seems dangerously one-sided, and in this one-sidedness threatens to re-enforce the very attitudes which underlie the practice of abortion since it is just a too avid and unmoderated sense of the value of my life (mistaking a penultimate for an ultimate good, in Bonhoeffer's terms) which motivates its protection at whatever cost, moral or otherwise.

One should not suppose that the best thing would be to position oneself between the advocates of a right to choose and the right to life (as self-proclaimed 'moderates' might conceive of themselves as doing). Placing oneself here may perhaps generate a certain sense of virtue since one can persuade oneself that one thereby partakes both of the fidelity to tradition which seems (but perhaps only seems) to belong to those who proclaim a right to life and also of the open-mindedness and sophistication which seems (but only seems) to belong to those who proclaim a right to choose. But however that may be, the intellectual merits of this position are non-existent, since it does not represent a higher and principled synthesis of these two positions but a mere averaging of them in a refusal to make a judgement. There is nothing to commend such a stance to Christian thought, which far from seeking to stand between these two positions, should consider whether it must actually stand outside and over this particular dialectic with its danger of presenting false options, bearing witness to its own distinctive perspective.

A community which knows human life to be created, reconciled and redeemed in Jesus Christ will be a community which, in its acceptance of children, gives expression to its characteristic virtues of faith, hope and love. With faith in the goodness of God's creation, a hope in his providential dealings with it, and a love appropriate to his regard for it, such a community would welcome children with a simplicity which is presupposed by Bonhoeffer's quick way with abortion. Once we have grasped this perspective, we can understand the very obviousness, as Bonhoeffer saw it, of the simple view and, furthermore, can understand the force of traditional Roman Catholic teaching in relation to certain hard cases.

According to that teaching abortion is always wrong, though an action which will result in the destruction of the foetus may sometimes be licit since it is permissible, for sufficient reason, to perform an action in itself good or indifferent, which has a bad result which is foreseen, but not intended. Thus, it would be licit for therapeutic reasons to remove a cancerous womb, even though this will result in the death of a foetus. In his recent encyclical letter *Evangelium Vitae* Pope John Paul II has reaffirmed this teaching, saying that 'direct abortion, that is, abortion willed as an end or as a means, always constitutes a grave moral disorder'.[2]

Let us imagine a case, however – it does not matter if it is uncommon or even unheard of, since its point is simply to display the presuppositions and implications of the teaching – in which mother and child will both die unless the foetus is aborted but which differs from the case described in the previous paragraph in one particular respect. In this second case no other medical condition intervenes, so that if the death of the foetus is brought about, it will be directly intended, since it is the means of saving the mother's life, and not, as where the cancerous womb is removed, a foreseen but unintended side effect of standardly indicated medical treatment. Now this difference, on this view, makes all the difference, so that in the second case the removal of the foetus from the womb would be regarded as wrong. Of course the motives for such an action would be good ones, namely to save the one life which can be saved from the tragic situation which is about to unfold. But, to revert to our earlier language, this would amount to the doing of evil that good may come and this is illicit. There is a slogan which sums up the judgement in this case, which has a harsh ring to it but reveals the logic of the thinking plainly enough – 'better two deaths than one murder'.[3]

Any quick and ready dismissal of this view betokens a failure to grasp its philosophical and Christian seriousness. Philosophically, the doctrine in virtue of which the distinction between the two cases is made, the so-called doctrine of double effect, is one which has been and would be defended by any number of philosophers, with or without Roman Catholic convictions. Why? – because the doctrine represents an attempt to distinguish between the different sorts of responsibility which may attach to intended as against foreseen consequences or side effects, and some such distinction is arguably presupposed in the rejection of consequentialism and hence in the respect for those patterns of moral thought which motivate that rejection. But a summary dismissal of Roman teaching can also be accused of shallowness from a Christian viewpoint. Suppose a woman took the view that she could not and would not ask a doctor to kill her child either in the case we have imagined (where, as a result, she and the child will die) or in the case where the refusal of an abortion will preserve the life of the child at the cost of her own. Is such a woman making a mistake of so crass a kind that we can dismiss her decision out of hand? Can we not understand the horror she might feel at laying a hand on her child, even if her unwillingness to consent to its being killed will result in the child's death and her own? If, without any false sentimentality, she feels herself called to express and witness to her commitment to this one who is her particular neighbour in this way, are we to say that she is quite simply and in a rather obvious way wrong? If we do say this – and a large number of Christians seem inclined to say it in their unthinking scorn of Roman Catholic teaching – we might just wonder whether we should not pause and try, perhaps with the help of a few novels if the Bible seems too distant, to enter the thought-world of those who actually believe that there are things worth dying for.

To find the Roman Catholic view philosophically and Christianly serious, however, is not the same as endorsing it without qualification. For just as we can find a certain cogency in this position, so we can find a cogency and seriousness in other analyses of the situation in which the continuation of the pregnancy threatens the death of both mother and child, or of one or other. There are two lines of thought which are deserving of consideration, even if both need in turn to be subject to further questioning.

In the first place, although a foetus is not plausibly regarded as an aggressor (supposing that an aggressor is one who intends harm), none the less it may be that the general permissibility of acting in self-defence is of some relevance here. It might be maintained, for example, that the legitimacy of self-defence extends not only to those who threaten our lives intentionally, but also to those who endanger them unintentionally or inadvertently, and perhaps especially where the death of the unintending aggressor is in any case certain no matter what I do. Of course, to say that such action in self-defence might be legitimate is not to say that a woman who declined to act in self-defence would be blameworthy, for the consequence of recognising the Christian seriousness of traditional Roman teaching is to acknowledge the seriousness of such a refusal. It is to say, however, that the point of view here entertained – that the choice of the life of the mother over the life of the child where the latter poses a threat to the former – is not morally forbidden, even if it is not morally required, and has a claim to be taken seriously alongside the Roman Catholic position. (It should perhaps, be pointed out, that one ought not to accept attempts to enlarge this class of cases by those expansive construals of the notion of 'posing a threat to the life of' which are employed on behalf of the status quo as regards abortion; a literal construal of the notion has the distinct merit of allowing us to see what it is about these cases which causes us a sense of difficulty, namely that like is pitted against like. But once we replace cases of life against life with cases of life against economic well-being, for example, the particular difficulty and poignancy of the situation is lost, and with it the particular force which this line of thinking might be reckoned to have.)

While the attempt to think through these cases in terms suggested by discussions of self-defence is worthy of careful examination, it is equally worthy of note that this line of thought may approach somewhat too closely reasoning of a sort we have earlier found wanting. The difficulty does not lie in those cases where the lives of mother and child will both be lost if action is not taken which could at least save the life of the mother; in those cases reasoning along the lines we have considered seems appropriate. The difficulty lies with those cases where only one or other could be saved. To bring into the consideration of such cases arguments having to do with rights to self-defence is once again to invite their treatment in terms appropriate to conflict resolution rather than to the relations of parent and child. It would be, as Luther might have it, to appeal to the laws which are made for the government of the earthly kingdom but have no place in the life of Christians, each one of whom is called to be – in his almost impious phrase – 'a Christ to my neighbour'.[4]

An alternative and better way of approaching these cases is suggested by Oliver O'Donovan.[5] According to O'Donovan, what is in danger of being overlooked in the traditional Roman Catholic analysis is that death has entered the situation of itself, so to speak. Mother or child, or mother and child, will die, whatever now happens. The physician who aborts a foetus in this situation has not chosen death, but only on whom death will fall. In some cases where the physician chooses that death will fall on the child, it may be that this is the only possibility besides its falling on both. If, however, the death of both may be prevented by death falling on either, the choice between mother and child may make reference to criteria which would none the less never justify a choice of a course of action which would itself bring death into the situation. (Thus a physician might properly have regard to the mother's role, obligations and duties in saving the mother and not the child where one or other must die, even though, as we have argued, a regard for these factors would never warrant the choosing of abortion where death was not already present.) Nor need a regard to these features of the situation be unworthy in the mind of the mother, who as well as considering her call to be Christ to this neighbour, may have other neighbours to whom she already has such a vocation. Of course, she may still choose that the child's life should be preferred to her own where only one may be saved. But whether she makes this or the other choice, both seem choices which are explicable in Christian terms.

IV. Aspects of a Genealogy of the Practice of Abortion

According to our argument thus far, society discusses abortion in ways which Christian thought cannot simply accept. To conceive this debate, as it typically is, as one concerning the right to choose or the right to life, creates a danger of its being misconceived. Bonhoeffer's simple view of these matters, so we have said, does not emerge from this debate, but presupposes a perspective outside it. But this perspective is the perspective on human life which comes from the gospel, in which it is learnt that human life needs no further justification than the justification it has from God. Thus though Christians may properly engage with the secular debate in an *ad hoc* and a pragmatic way – and indeed ought to do so insofar as this engagement may demonstrate some of the confusions and inadequacies of that debate even in its own terms and in so doing may encourage a questioning of current practice – they will do so knowing that the simple view will only gain understanding and acceptance as the Christian gospel is itself understood and accepted.

There is one aspect of a pragmatic and *ad hoc* engagement with the current debate which we have not yet discussed, however, and which we cannot pass over just because it seems so unjustly neglected. Though we have set out in the first section of this essay some of the questions which a critic might pose in the current debate without, as it were, going outside it, there are further points which might be put by the same critic not so much *within* the debate as *about* it and which may do something more to put it in question.

One distinct oddity of the debate about abortion lies in the relation which this debate seems to bear (or, in fact, not to bear) to practice, for the fact is that the practice seems independent of the argument. We should be precise about what we mean here. It is, of course, possible, as we have allowed, that arguments could be advanced in favour of current practice which would be perfectly consistent and, furthermore, might proceed from premises which could not be shown simply and uncontroversially to be wrong. The point now, however, is not to contest that claim, but to suggest that even if such a case has been made or could be made in principle, present practice has not obviously arisen out of any such arguments. Three aspects of the present situation seem to support this contention and we shall have to content ourselves with mentioning them, rather than developing them as fully as they might and ought to be.

In the first place, Noonan's claim of nearly thirty years ago – that there is a distinct 'indifference to fundamental questions' in public discussion of abortion – certainly seems to hold good now.[1] A telling sign is the fact that one would search the *Warnock Report* in vain for arguments to support the view that fourteen days is a morally significant moment in the development of the embryo, even though the Report claims to 'have attempted to argue in favour of those positions we have adopted' and even though this particular 'position' is central to the Report's recommendation in favour of the practice of experimentation.[2]

In the second place and following on from this point, we have already had occasion to notice that the practice of most Western jurisdictions presents, prima facie, something of a muddle in protecting the embryo from experimentation after fourteen days whilst offering no protection to the foetus in the womb for the subsequent twenty-two weeks or so. It would not be impossible to construct an argument to defend this dichotomy, but it is likely to require mental gymnastics of a fairly high order. On the face of it, argument is more likely to condemn rather than excuse current practice in this regard, and even if it didn't, the argument which would provide the apology would be, as our last point suggested, *ex post facto*.

In the third place, let us note another respect in which the practice seems unrelated to argument. If our review of the debate in its own terms has suggested anything, it has suggested something of the difficulty of the issue judged from within that frame of reference – it would be only the most dogmatic of defenders of the status quo who could declare that the foetus is, without a shadow of doubt, unworthy of moral regard or consideration. But if that is so, were current practice to reflect the state of argument, we would expect it to be somewhat tentative and hesitant, whereas what we find is a rather confident, clear-cut and decisive practice, the routinisation of which effectively denies the existence of moral difficulties regarding abortion. The practice seems to presuppose, that is to say, that the case for the acceptability of abortion is beyond any reasonable debate, whereas a review of the arguments in their own terms hardly suggests the possibility of such absolute conviction.

Just because it seems, for these three reasons, that the practice sits somewhat free of argument we may feel encouraged to ask a question which would not be inappropriate even if we had found a tight fit between argument and practice, but which seems especially appropriate here. What has driven the emergence of this practice in the modern West? We have spent some time considering what arguments might be constructed by way of justification for abortion, and have not only found most of the arguments wanting, but have said furthermore that, however one judges these arguments, they do not seem to have functioned as the basis for the practice. We might be led to suspect, then, that what has driven the practice are not arguments which declare that it is legitimate to meet the need for abortion, or to kill unwanted children, or to take the lives of those whose lives will be burdensome to them, or whatever, but rather the prior perceptions of a need for abortion, of the existence of unwanted children and burdensome life, and so on. (After all, we could imagine a culture which would be perplexed by the question whether it is permissible to kill unwanted children just because it finds the category of 'unwanted children' to be empty.) Reason has been overwhelmed, we might say, by categorisations, attitudes and expectations which are not themselves necessarily the children of reason, but products of diverse social forces – in the same way, argument about euthanasia may find itself simply overwhelmed by a culture which leads the elderly to identify themselves as 'a drain on scarce resources', to think of dependence on care as 'undignified' and to regard any death which is not self-willed and controlled as 'demeaning'. In these circumstances, discussion about the propriety of doctors taking patients' lives will go on at the margins.

To venture an account of the genesis of the categorisations, attitudes and expectations associated with the practice of abortion is quite beyond this essay. But any such genealogy is likely to make reference to one important factor in the shaping of present mentalities which it is appropriate to pick out for mention here, even if we cannot complete the picture, for the sake of beginning to dispel the innocence of treatments of abortion which deal only with the world of reason. And we can get at this factor by looking at Friedrich Engels' early and important work *The Condition of the Working Class in England*.

As Engels sees it the life of society has become, in fact, nothing of the kind. Instead 'isolation of the individual, ... narrow self-seeking, is the fundamental principle of our society everywhere', though it is 'nowhere so shamelessly barefaced, so self-conscious as just here in the crowding of the great city. The dissolution of mankind into monads, of which each one has a separate essence, and a separate purpose, the world of atoms, is here carried out to its utmost extreme.'[3] And it is carried to this extreme under the compulsion of the development of capitalism, for which competition – the 'war of each against all'[4] – is the normal and proper condition of human life. But note, the development of capitalism creates not only a more perfect form of the competition of social classes, though it does indeed do that in securing the existence of the proletariat as a class of wage-labourers and of the bourgeoisie as the class of those who exploit such labourers; also and importantly the development of capitalism comes to determine the form and character of relationships within these classes. Engels writes:

> Competition is the completest expression of the battle of all against all which rules in modern civil society. This battle, a battle for life, for existence, for everything, in case of need a battle for life and death, is fought not between the different classes of society only, but also between the individual members of these classes. Each is in the way of the other, and each seeks to crowd out all who are in his way, and to put himself in their place. The workers are in constant competition among themselves as the members of the bourgeoisie among themselves. The power-loom weaver is in competition with the hand-loom weaver, the unemployed or ill-paid hand-loom weaver with the man who has work or is better paid, each trying to supplant the other.[5]

Thus 'In this country, social war is under full headway, every one stands for himself, and fights for himself against all comers, and whether or not he shall injure all the others who are his declared foes, depends upon a cynical calculation as to what is most advantageous for himself.'[6] Nor, by the way, should we expect the State to represent a real bar or check to 'social war': 'Free competition will suffer no limitation, no State supervision; the whole State is a burden to it. It would reach its highest perfection in a wholly ungoverned anarchic society, where each might exploit the other to his heart's content.'[7]

Now what the State will not check, the workers try to

oppose; the workers, according to Engels, attempt to nullify this 'competition ... among themselves' through association; 'hence the hatred of the bourgeoisie towards these associations, and its triumph in every defeat which befalls them.'[8] But such association takes other forms than nascent trade unions, and these others are no less a bar to the perfect and complete 'competition of workers among themselves' and thus no less subject to attack as the demands of competition are extended. These demands, for example, fuel, so Engels thought, the dissolution of the family which is achieved in a variety of ways: in the employment of children; in the necessity for women to work, and to work immediately prior to and straight after childbirth; in the high unemployment of men, and so on. And this dissolution of the family and of the community of interest which it represents is strikingly symbolised in a detail of working-class life in respect of children's dealings with their parents: 'When they get on far enough to earn more than they cost their parents from week to week, they begin to pay their parents a fixed sum for board and lodging, and keep the rest for themselves. This often happens from the fourteenth or fifteenth year. In a word, the children emancipate themselves, and regard the paternal dwelling as a lodging house, which they often exchange for another as suits them.'[9]

The forces of competition reach even here then, destroying this association and the community of interest which it sustains just as surely as it seeks the destruction of other associations. The imperative to treat the other as 'mere material, a mere chattel'[10] touches even the family, recreating it in a form which meets the needs of competition.

We can hardly read this analysis of the outworking of the logic of capitalism through the reordering of the structure of social relations, including the social relations of the family, without being struck by the possibility of extending Engels' analysis to those developments in the form of the family with which we have been concerned. Where competition provides a dominant structure of social relations, and the 'war of each against all' is more and more generalised, and where the view of the other as a 'mere material, a mere chattel' is a presupposition and a consequence of these social relations, the fact that an unborn child can come to be thought of as a threat and a stranger should hardly surprise us. The family must bow to the needs of competition, and be fashioned by it, so that the practice of abortion, it might be claimed, is the practice of competition, borne not of the logic of argument but of the logic of capitalism.

Of course, that such an analysis would have a part to play in a larger and more complete genealogy is here simply suggested, as we have said, without being established – nor have we begun to discuss the sort of qualifications and amendments which we might want to add to Engels' rather stylised picture. The important point is, however, that the refusal of most discussions of abortion even to entertain such a genealogy gives them an overly intellectualist character, since they seem to believe, in effect, that social relations, modern Western medicine, the family and the like, are touched by nothing as base as economic forces, but have their character in virtue of pure reason. (Perhaps we should note in passing, too, how often in these same discussions 'feelings' enter as an authentic and original datum which might serve as an arbiter in the debate, as if 'feelings' also stand outside the stream of history and social life.) We might find ourselves led to the view that the real genius of capitalism lies not so much in fashioning the social world as it sees fit, nor even in persuading women to think that the dissolution of bonds of sympathy between children and parents, and indeed between parents, represents in some sense their liberation. Its real genius lies in concealing this achievement almost entirely from view. Christianity will bring this achievement out into the open, and in so doing will finally subsume any genealogy of the kind which it finds in Engels, even as it is willing to learn from it, in a richer and more fundamental genealogy of human alienation from God. In doing so, however, it too will place abortion in a social context which will be known as standing in need of a genuine liberation.

V. What About the Law?

Even if with Engels we do not expect that the law will stand effectively in the way of the generalising of competition, still we must turn to the question of what the law ought or ought not to allow as regards abortion. It might be thought, however, that an answer to that question follows very quickly from what we have thus far said, but the matter is not quite so simple.

In general terms, from the fact that one takes the view that something is morally wrong, it does not follow immediately and without further argument that the law should take any note of it, and even where it should, it is by no means obvious what this 'taking note' – we use that phrase advisedly – should consist in. Greed, for example, is probably a vice more vicious than many others, but not obviously one the incidence of which the law could or should endeavour to affect. And even of a vice of which it is agreed that the law could and should take note, the form in which it should do so can be a matter of considerable difficulty and dispute. Take prostitution. If the law is to take a critical view of prostitution that view could be expressed in diverse ways. The law could provide for the punishment of prostitutes and their clients; it might punish neither of these, but only those who live off the proceeds of prostitution; there again it might punish no one at all, but could refuse to enforce any contracts for prostitution; or, to mention another possible option, with or without the last measure, it could simply express its disapproval by prohibiting the advertisement of prostitution.

The subtleties of whether and how the law might take note of the practice of abortion are often lost in popular debate, where a couple of suppositions seem unaffected by their doing without much in the way of argumentative support. The first supposition is that if the generality of abortions are morally wrong the law should certainly take note of abortions, and the second is that if it should take note of them it should do so in the very specific sense of criminalising abortion (though it may be unclear whether it is those who seek or those who perform abortions, or both, who are to be subject to the criminal law). Our point has been that the first conclusion really ought to be a conclusion, and that the second ignores the many options which lie between a studied neutrality and an outright criminalising of those seeking or performing abortions. The falsity of these options adds to the unreality of the debate, since those who argue for neutrality usually argue against criminalisation, whereas those who argue for criminalisation usually argue against neutrality – and this, to many, will seem like a choice between the devil and the deep blue sea.

The exact form in which the law should take note of abortion, supposing that it should take note in some way, is not a matter which can be pursued here since, as the above example of prostitution must make clear, the final determination of this matter involves the consideration and weighing of a multiplicity of factors. But since we are inclined to the view that the law should in some form or other take note of it, we have to deal with three considerations (they are not really well formed enough to be counted as arguments) which are often used against this claim and to support the status quo.

The first consideration points to the very widespread acceptance of abortion which has either grown up since or been revealed by the reform of the law. In England and Wales some 180,000 abortions were performed in 1996.[1] In the United States it is estimated that as many as 1,500,000 abortions take place annually. Thus in these jurisdictions a very large number of women indeed will have an abortion in the course of their lives. Supposing, as is probably reasonable, that in many of these cases the women will have the support of their partners (though one must allow for the fact that some may be acting solely in deference to their partners' wishes), friends or family members, it seems to follow that a very sizeable portion of the population has come to regard abortion as a service which should be generally available. We may also suppose that of those who have not and will not have abortions, none the less a good number take the same view. Is it conceivable, then, that the law could act (in whatever way) against what is now so widely regarded as a right? Wouldn't any step towards criminalisation of abortions – even in relation to what we might think of as eugenic abortions on grounds of sex, for example – be so contentious given the strength of feelings on this matter, that a state which attempted to go in this direction would at the least bring the law into disrepute (since the criminalisation of abortion would, like the criminalisation of smoking on the streets of Paris, be effectively unenforceable), and might at the worst provoke civil disobedience and conflict?

A second consideration has to do with the situation which obtained before the reform of the law. Prior to the decriminalising of abortion, abortions still went on, but in a way which was, from any point of view, highly undesirable. Women were prey to unscrupulous and often unqualified back-street abortionists, whose lack of skill increased the risks of abortion and who had no interest in providing the counselling which might have led some women to decide against abortion. Thus criminalisation not only failed to prevent abortions, it may even have served in some cases to encourage them, and certainly it meant that whatever abortions were performed were performed in a way which no one could think acceptable.

A third consideration relates to the first, and maintains that any attempt to change the legally permissive view is in some sense undemocratic or unjust. This charge seems to allege one or other or both of two things. It may mean to maintain that since the majority view is that abortion should be permissible without let or hindrance, any view to the contrary, while it has a perfect right to a hearing, can have no right to seek to affect the legal situation prior to a shift in popular views. But it might be a bit stronger than that, since the point just made concedes that in principle a State could determine to prohibit abortion if there was majority support for such a prohibition, whereas some would want to claim that the State has no such prerogative. No one should be obliged to have an abortion, they might say, but equally no one should be prevented from having one. It is a matter of personal choice with which the State should not interfere. Hence the law should simply be neutral on the matter.

Looking back at these arguments we might represent them as maintaining that it would be impossible for the law to act against the availability of abortion, or if not impossible then undesirable in practice, or if not undesirable in practice then wrong in principle. We should say something about each of these, taking them in reverse order.

The last argument – which says that it would be undemocratic to change the law without majority support, or, more strongly that even a majority would behave wrongly in amending the law – claims too much, or at least plainly relies on arguments of the sort we have encountered earlier and cannot simply be dependent on supposed truths of political theory. The point, to be blunt, is that the case for a prohibition of slavery, for example, would not be weakened by the observation that no one is compelled to keep slaves. If abortion is morally wrong, for reasons we have entertained, then the interest which the law may properly take in abortion is the interest it has in relation to slavery or infanticide. Of course there is disagreement, as we have said, as to whether abortion is a wrongful attack on life or not, and if it is not, then certainly the law has no obvious business in taking a view of it. But the proposition that the law has no business with abortion depends on the proposition that it is not a wrongful attack on life, and cannot be established simply by reflection on the limits of State power (unless, that is, one makes a case for the merits of anarchism).

If the law is entitled to an interest in the matter, would it be inadvisable, or indeed impossible, for it to alter the present practice as the first two considerations suggest? It is worth pointing out before saying anything else that the inadvisability or impossibility which is suggested here is in actual fact the inadvisability or impossibility of a regime of rather direct, simple and perhaps highly punitive criminalisation, whereas we have already suggested that the reform of the law allows any number of options between punishing those who seek or provide abortions and simple neutrality. Thus whatever force these arguments have against any move to criminalisation, they obviously possess much lesser force, or even none, in relation to these other options.

But putting that highly important qualification to one side for the moment, let us consider what significance we should attach to the possible consequences of a change in the law which involved criminalisation. Remember that there were two points here – either that such a change would be, from any point of view, undesirable as resulting in higher maternal mortality without necessarily reducing (and possibly even increasing) the number of abortions, or if not undesirable in these terms, such as to bring the law into disrepute or to provoke mass civil disobedience because unenforceable and highly contentious.

The empirical judgements on which such claims depend are plainly difficult to substantiate, but for the sake of argument let us allow that they have a degree of plausibility. Should those who think abortion a wrong in some respects on a par with infanticide desist from any attempt at criminalisation in view of these scenarios, in one of which the numbers of abortions is unaffected and the suffering of women is increased, and in the other of which there is a breakdown in respect for the law going so far, perhaps, as to threaten the civil order? Grim as these possibilities are, it is by no means obvious how one should respond. Consider a parallel case. Suppose we take the view that discrimination on grounds of race is wrong, but recognise that in some societies it is deeply engrained. Imagine a move to criminalise it were met with bleak scenarios – an attempt to criminalise racial discrimination will have no obvious effect on its incidence and may even increase it since the passage of legislation could itself become a focus for resentment of minority populations; it may even be that this resentment will run so deep as to provoke blatant challenges to the State and its power and perhaps even violence towards minority groups. What should be done? Cases could be made for or against the passage of legislation, but at the least it is not obvious that the case against the legislation and in favour of the status quo is overwhelming. After all, one might be led to reflect in relation to the most extreme scenario, that the break-down in the rule of law which is predicted could be regarded as a simple revelation of what is already in fact the case. As Augustine wrote:

> Remove justice and what are kingdoms but gangs of crim-inals on a large scale? ... For it was a witty and a truthful rejoinder which was given by a captured pirate to Alexander the Great. The king asked the fellow, 'What is your idea, in infesting this sea?' And the pirate answered, with uninhibited insolence, 'The same as yours, in infesting the earth! But because I do it with a tiny craft, I'm called a pirate: because you have a mighty navy, you're called an emperor.'[2]

Piracy is a bad thing, but not obviously worse than State pira-cy; or, to put it simply, a rule of law which fails to protect the lives and rights of certain classes of a nation's citizens (be they the unborn or racial minorities) is as partial a rule of law as that which civil disobedience is itself likely to threaten.

VI. Conclusion

Whilst Christians quite properly have a concern for the provisions of the criminal law, it would be unrealistic to imagine that any likely or even conceivable changes in the law could serve of themselves to reverse the ever increasing resort to abortion in Western countries. Nor, if our analysis is right, is argument likely of itself to succeed where legal reform would fail.

According to Bonhoeffer in his rather dire circumstances, in meeting the threats to the simple Christian view not only of abortion but of human life and existence in general, Christians had to take up the 'sharp swords' of simplicity and wisdom – the first consists in fixing 'one's eye solely on the simple truth of God at a time when all concepts are being confused, distorted and turned upside down.' And 'simplicity becomes wisdom', since 'the wise man is the one who sees reality as it is, and who sees into the depths of things. That is why only that man is wise who sees reality in God.'[1] But this, of course, is, for Bonhoeffer, to see reality in Jesus Christ: 'It is in Jesus Christ that God's relation to the world is defined. We know of no relation of God to the world other than through Jesus Christ.'[2]

A Church which saw reality through Jesus Christ would witness to the world through a way of life which would express those truths about human existence, its origin and its destiny, which are known in him. This way of life, in what is done as much as in what is said, would be welcoming of children, female as well as male, handicapped as well as unhandicapped, planned as well as unplanned. Such a way of life would find expression in countless practical endeavours, just as Christian witness always has, to support and assist those who are seeking to live the life of discipleship to which the Gospel calls us, aware as Bonhoeffer put it, that guilt in these matters 'may often lie rather with the community than with the individual'. In that life of discipleship there would be nothing of the despising of human existence, the despair in its course, and the estrangement of one from another, which presently characterise our dealings with the unborn, but not only the unborn. Instead, where there is faith, hope and love, there would be a life of joy in which abortion would not first of all be thought wrong, but would be quite simply, as Bonhoeffer says, unthinkable.

Questions

I Introduction

1. What is your present reaction to Bonhoeffer's view that it is a 'simple fact' that abortion is 'nothing but murder'?
2. The author states his view that the way abortion is usually discussed ignores or bypasses a specifically Christian viewpoint. Do you agree?

II The Current Debate

(a) Does the Status of the Foetus Matter?

1. Some people justify abortion on the grounds of 'consequentialist' arguments – i.e. the view that the end justifies the means. In which cases, at present, would you think abortion justified?
   (a) The case of a teenager who has been raped?
   (b) The case of a young married couple expecting a child earlier than they had intended?
   (c) The case of a couple expecting a child with a minor handicap (e.g. harelip)?
   (d) The case of a couple expecting a child with a more significant handicap (e.g. Down's Syndrome)?
   (e) The case of a couple expecting a child of one sex when the other was preferred?
2. If you believe that a foetus known to be handicapped may be aborted, where will you draw the line on how severe must the handicap be?
3. How far would you agree with the author that the 'consequentialist' calculation involved in these decisions is uncertain, and likely to be affected by the particular character and temperament of the people involved?

4. From a Christian perspective, how much should our own wishes count in making such a decision?
5. Can you think of examples where one might properly do an evil act so that good may come from it?
6. Which, if any, kinds of evil action are always ruled out? How does killing the foetus compare with these?
7. Do you agree with the author's view that 'a woman's right to choose' could be a mere slogan employed to evade moral argument?

(b) What Is the Status of the Foetus?
1. What exceptions would you allow to the principle 'thou shalt not kill'? On what grounds?
2. The present law excludes a foetus of up to twenty-four weeks from the scope of the protection laid down by the principle 'thou shalt not kill'. Do you agree that there are grounds for doing so?
3. How would you answer the question, 'Is the foetus a person?'
4. Is there greater justification for killing the foetus, which will eventually possess all the faculties needed for a full human life, than those for killing the severely mentally handicapped or senile who have permanently lost those faculties?
5. What do you think of the arguments in favour of the present law which allows abortion up to the presumed time of 'viability' (twenty-four weeks)?
6. How do you rate the argument that the non-sentience (inability to feel pain) of the foetus justifies abortion?
7. The present law permits experimentation on live human embryos up to fourteen days. What do you think of the arguments used to justify this, and those of the author to oppose it?
8. Since the law forbids experimentation on live human embryos after fourteen days, is it logical that it also permits their destruction up to twenty-four weeks?

9. Do you think the author has successfully shown that there are no moral grounds justifying the exclusion of the foetus from the protection we otherwise afford to human life?

III Beyond the Current Debate

1. The author believes that Christians are wrong to argue against abortion on the grounds of the unborn child's 'right to life', because he believes that framing the discussion in terms of a woman's 'right to choose' versus the unborn child's 'right to life' shows a fundamentally un-Christian perspective on the issue. What is your view?
2. Are you convinced by the moral distinction which the author draws between (a) removing the cancerous womb of a pregnant mother, thus saving the life of the mother but entailing, inevitably but unintentionally, the death of the foetus; and (b) performing an abortion to save the mother in a case where both mother and foetus will die if the pregnancy goes to term? Does there seem to you to be an important moral distinction between an action with a directly intended result, and an action with a foreseen, but not directly intended one?
3. How right, in Christian terms, are the instincts of a mother who refuses an abortion (a) in a case where it is clear that both she and the foetus will die if the pregnancy goes to term; and (b) in a case where an abortion would save her own life?

IV Aspects of a Genealogy of the Practice of Abortion

1. Do you agree that there is 'a distinct indifference to fundamental questions' in public discussion of abortion?
2. Do you agree with the author that the practice of abortion is at least partly linked to the force of competitive selfishness in our social system? To what else would you attribute the change of attitude which has taken place this century?

V What About the Law?

1. What do you make of the views (a) that it would now be impracticable to recriminalise abortion? and (b) that it would be undesirable or wrong in principle to do so?
2. How strong an argument is it against the recriminalisation of abortion to say that it would make women once again resort to back-street abortionists?

VI Conclusion

1. Do you agree with the author about what a specifically Christian view of abortion would be?
2. How has this booklet affected your view of the moral issues surrounding the practice of abortion?

Notes

I. Introduction

1. D. Bonhoeffer, *Ethics*, tr. N. H. Smith (London, 1955), 149-50.

II. The Current Debate

1. Augustine, *Against Lying*, tr. H. Browne in *The Nicene and Post-Nicene Fathers*, first series, vol. iii (Edinburgh, 1988).
2. Augustine, *Against Lying*, 487.
3. The reader is asked to note that the use of irony is not forbidden ministers of the Church of England.
4. The variety of moral claims is brought out tellingly in Mary Midgeley's 'Duties Concerning Islands' in *Environmental Ethics*, ed. R. Elliott (Oxford, 1995), 89-103.
5. See, for some of the issues, the Parliamentary Office of Science and Technology's 'Fetal Awareness', P.O.S.T. note 94 (London, 1997).
6. J. Rachels, *Created From Animals: The Moral Implications of Darwinism* (Oxford, 1990), 5. For Nietzsche on this theme see *The Anti-Christ*, tr. R. J. Hollingdale (Harmondsworth, 1968).
7. K. Barth, *Church Dogmatics*, III/2, tr. H. Knight *et al.* (Edinburgh, 1960), 228.

III. Beyond the Current Debate

1. K. Barth, *Church Dogmatics*, III/4, tr. A.T. Mackay *et al.* (Edinburgh, 1961), 326.
2. John Paul II, *Evangelium Vitae*, English translation (London, 1995), 62.
3. Readers should be aware that though I have given a standard account of the doctrine of double effect, the noted Roman Catholic moral theologian Germain Grisez has a different interpretation dependent in turn on a different analysis of action. This allows him to offer solutions to the difficult cases discussed distinct from those normally found in the Roman Catholic tradition, and similar in many respects to those given. See G. Grisez, *Living a Christian Life*, vol. 2 of *The Way of the Lord Jesus* (Quincy, IU., 1993), 469-74 and 500-4.
4. M. Luther, *The Freedom of a Christian*, in many editions.
5. O.M.T. O'Donovan, *The Christian and the Unborn Child*, second edi-

tion (Bramcote, Notts., 1975).

IV. Aspects of a Genealogy of the Practice of Abortion

1. J.T. Noonan (ed.), *The Morality of Abortion* (Cambridge, Mass., 1970), 'Introduction', xviii.
2. *Report of the Committee of Inquiry into Human Fertilisation and Embryology, 'The Warnock Report'* (London, 1984), paragraph 2.
3. F. Engels, *The Condition of the Working Class in England*, translation of 1886 revised (Harmondsworth, 1987), 69.
4. ibid., 142.
5. ibid., 111.
6. ibid., 156.
7. ibid., 276.
8. ibid., 112.
9. ibid., 167.
10. ibid., 92.

V. What About the Law?

1. *Britain, 1998: An Official Handbook*, The Office of National Statistics (London, 1998).
2. Augustine, *City of God*, tr. H. Bettenson (Harmondsworth, 1972), iv, 4.

VI. Conclusion

1. Bonhoeffer, op. cit., 50.
2. ibid., 321.